THE STRESS LESS GUIDE

SOCIAL MEDIA MARKETING MADE EASY

Published by eMarketing Director LLC

TABLE OF CONTENTS

THIS WORKBOOK WAS MADE FOR YOU TO WRITE ON, USE, ERASE, TRY AGAIN, AND KEEP GOING. THE WORKBOOK IS DIVIDED INTO 8 SECTIONS. TO GET THE MOST OUT OF THIS WORKBOOK, START WITH SECTION 1 AND 2 AND THEN CHOOSE WHAT YOU WANT TO DO IN SECTIONS 3 THROUGH 7. SECTION 8 PROVIDES EXAMPLES TO SEE THE WORKBOOK IN ACTION.

Managing Your Marketing Stress

Welcome to the eMarketing Director workbook, Social Media Marketing Made Easy. This workbook is for anyone who wants to add more organization to their social media marketing for their company, their nonprofit, or themselves if they want to be an influencer. By completing this workbook, you are striving to manage the stress that marketing creates for anyone wanting to sell a product or service or collect donations by organizing and planning your social media marketing ahead of schedule. You can stress less by using this workbook to help you make a plan and stick to it to further automate your social media marketing. You can think less about the online clutter and more about meeting your goals, gaining a return on investment, and getting back to doing the things you love. Let's get started!

PURPOSE

STEP ONE

COMMIT TO COMPLETING THE WORKBOOK. THIS WORKBOOK WAS DEVELOPED TO HELP YOU BE LESS STRESSED, SO CREATE A REGULAR SCHEDULE TO REVIEW THESE MATERIALS.

STEP TWO

ACKNOWLEDGE THE STRESS THAT SOCIAL MEDIA MARKETING CREATES. IT IS STRESSFUL TO BE A MARKETER! BUT BY ORGANIZING AND PLANNING, YOU'LL GAIN KNOWLEDGE AND CONFIDENCE IN YOUR CAMPAIGNS AND CONTENT.

STEP THREE

DETERMINE WHAT YOU HAVE UPFRONT. USE THE CHECKLISTS IN THIS WORKBOOK TO ASSESS WHAT YOU HAVE NOW, SO YOU KNOW WHAT YOU NEED TO DO NEXT.

STEP FOUR

PLAN AHEAD. USE THE CALENDARS AND BRAINSTORMING SPACES IN THIS WORKBOOK TO DETERMINE WHAT YOU NEED TO DO AND DECIDE HOW TO GET IT DONE QUICKLY AND EFFECTIVELY.

STEP FIVE

REFLECT ON WHAT IS NEXT. AS YOU COMPLETE YOUR CAMPAIGNS USE THE CHARTS AND NOTES TO REFLECT ON HOW TO GAIN MORE SUCCESS OVER TIME.

TIMELINE

YOUR NAME: _____

YOUR COMPANY/ORGANIZATION/PROJECT NAME: _____

STEP ONE

SET CLEAR GOALS. THINKING ABOUT WHAT YOU CAN ACHIEVE OVER TIME WILL KEEP YOU MOTIVATED! USE THE **GETTING STARTED** SECTION TO SET SPECIFIC AND REACHABLE GOALS FOR YOURSELF.

STEP TWO

ESTABLISH A SCHEDULE. DEDICATE A SPECIFIC DAY AND TIME OF THE WEEK TO REVIEW AND ADJUST YOUR PLANS IN YOUR WORKBOOK. USE THE **PLATFORM PLANNER** SECTION TO CREATE YOUR OWN PERSONALIZED TO-DO LIST.

STEP THREE

SHARE YOUR WORKBOOK WITH A COLLEAGUE, FRIEND, OR MENTOR WHO CAN GIVE YOU FEEDBACK. USE THE **SOCIAL MEDIA CAMPAIGN PLANNER, MONTHLY CONTENT PLANNER, AND YEARLY PLANNER** SECTION TO GUIDE YOUR CONVERSATIONS.

STEP FOUR

REWARD YOURSELF! CREATE A REWARD SYSTEM AND TREAT YOURSELF AS YOU MEET YOUR GOALS! USE THE **NOTES AND APPENDIX** SECTION TO REFLECT ON WHAT YOU'VE ACCOMPLISHED.

I WILL GET THE MOST OUT OF THIS WORKBOOK BY STICKING TO THE TIMELINE TO ORGANIZE AND PLAN MY SOCIAL MEDIA MARKETING!

WHAT IS STRESS?

Stress is a natural state, but it feels unnatural. Stress occurs as a reaction to challenges and changes. This can create a loop: the feeling of stress creates even more stress and then anxiety. When working in digital marketing, you will experience challenges and changes often. From the social media platforms introducing new features and sunsetting old features without warning, to the rise of AI, to the constant requirement of more and more content, feelings of stress are acceptable. By being mindful of the stress you may face, and preparing for the challenges and changes of digital marketing, you can be more aware of stress to try to stay cool in the moment and stick to your goals.

✔ **Who**

Stress can impact anyone and is a reaction to external circumstances, internal thoughts, and emotions.

✔ **What**

Stress can be felt in your body and in emotions. You may feel a rapid heartbeat, overwhelm, or tension.

✔ **When**

Stress can be situational, either acute or chronic, and occur during times of change and challenge.

✔ **Where**

Stress can happen at work, home, or school. It can also happen while you're online or offline.

✔ **Why**

Stress can be both external and internal. External causes may include budgets and deadlines. Internal causes may include self-expectations and mindset.

✔ **How**

Stress can be managed through practicing a mindfulness routine, preparing ahead of time, anticipating change and challenges, and seeking support.

DONE IS BETTER THAN PERFECT

01 You need marketing that makes a connection with people.

Perfect marketing doesn't exist. No marketing campaign or content is perfect. Instead, the goal is to connect with people (who are also not perfect) and help satisfy their wants or needs.

02 Recognize that perfection isn't the point.

There are several types of perfectionism. Sometimes it's motivating, but many times it hurts more than helps us. We can overcome perfectionism when we recognize that done is better than perfect and decide if our content meets our goals or not as our main benchmark for success.

03 Develop a system to move you forward.

Set up a system to help you move forward. Create and use rules to help you, for example: use the same photo editing settings, check writing for grammar, and make sure the video is to the point - then move forward.

04 Practice self-compassion to keep your stress levels down.

Be kind to yourself. Marketing is a hard job, often paired with many other responsibilities for a business or organization. You cannot control the Internet. You can only control what tasks you try to accomplish each day to move your work forward to reach your goals.

05 Make goals for yourself to grow.

Sometimes things don't go as planned. When reviewing your marketing, pay special attention to what went well (and celebrate!) but also decide what didn't go as well and write down what changes you can make in the future.

GETTING STARTED

checklists, brainstorming, goals, and more

A Little Planning
Goes a Long Way

One of the hardest things to do is "hurry up and wait." However, planning your social media marketing will give you the opportunity to align your goals with your business or organization's objectives and missions and give you something to measure to make sure you are reaching your goals. If you aren't reaching those goals, planning will help you determine what is missing and how to get back on track. Use this section to think about your goals and what you need to do before creating content and posting on your social media profiles.

VOCABULARY

THE FOLLOWING WORDS ARE USED THROUGHOUT THIS WORKBOOK. USE THIS AS A QUICK GUIDE AS YOU NAVIGATE YOUR SOCIAL MEDIA MARKETING.

01 SOCIAL MEDIA PLATFORM: ANY WEBSITE THAT CONNECTS YOU TO PEOPLE ONLINE TO SHARE INTERESTS AND ACTS AS A COMMUNITY.

02 SOCIAL MEDIA PROFILE: YOUR OWN SPACE ON A SOCIAL MEDIA PLATFORM, ALSO KNOWN AS A PAGE.

03 SOCIAL MEDIA POST: WRITTEN TEXT, PHOTOS, OR VIDEOS THAT ARE POSTED FOR THE PUBLIC OR YOUR FOLLOWERS TO SEE AND INTERACT WITH BY CLICKING ON A LINK OR SHARING IT.

04 AUDIENCE: PEOPLE WHO ARE ON SOCIAL MEDIA PLATFORMS, WHO MAY OR MAY NOT FOLLOW YOUR PROFILE, BUT WHO SEE YOUR CONTENT. THEY MAY BE YOUR CUSTOMERS OR POTENTIAL FUTURE CUSTOMERS.

05 NICHE: WHAT YOU DO BEST; YOUR INDUSTRY; YOUR AREA OF BUSINESS FOR YOUR PRODUCT, SERVICE, OR BRAND.

06 TAGS: TEXT THAT LINKS YOUR CONTENT TO ANOTHER PROFILE, LOCATION, OR TOPIC.

07 CALL TO ACTION: A SENTENCE OR PHRASE THAT TELLS YOUR AUDIENCE WHAT YOU WANT THEM TO DO. (I.E. CLICK ON THE LINK, SHOP NOW, SIGN UP.)

08 CAMPAIGNS VS CONTENT: CAMPAIGNS ARE THE OVERALL PLAN FOR HOW TO REACH YOUR GOAL. CONTENT IS THE INDIVIDUAL PHOTOS, VIDEOS AND TEXT THAT HELP YOU REACH YOUR GOAL.

START HERE

USE THE FOLLOWING PAGE TO QUICK START YOUR
EXPERIENCE WITH THIS WORKBOOK.

NAME OF MY BUSINESS /
ORGANIZATION -

What is being sold?

Who are you selling to?

Social Media Platforms My Audience
Uses (and I want to use them):

☐ _____

☐ _____

☐ _____

☐ _____

☐ _____

Social Media Platforms My Audience
Does Not Use (or ones I do not want to use):

☐ _____

☐ _____

☐ _____

☐ _____

☐ _____

How will I measure my success? What does success look like to me?

READY & SET CHECKLIST

THE FOLLOWING ARE THE BASICS YOU NEED AS YOU APPROACH SOCIAL MEDIA MARKETING. AS YOU READ EACH QUESTION, CHECK YES OR NO. IF YOU CHECK NO FOR ANYTHING, BE SURE TO ADD IT TO YOUR TO-DO LIST!

		YES	NO
01	DO YOU HAVE GOALS SET FOR YOUR SOCIAL MEDIA MARKETING THIS YEAR?	☐	☐
02	DO YOU HAVE PROFILES ON AT LEAST 1-3 PLATFORMS FOR YOUR SOCIAL MEDIA MARKETING AND DO YOU HAVE CURRENT USERNAME AND PASSWORD INFORMATION FOR EACH PROFILE?	☐	☐
03	HAVE YOU CHECKED YOUR PLATFORM AD MANAGERS AND SETTINGS TO ENSURE NO PREVIOUS EMPLOYEES OR INTERNS STILL HAVE ACCESS?	☐	☐
04	DO YOU HAVE AN APPROVED BUDGET SET UP FOR ADVERTISING ON THE PROFILES?	☐	☐
05	DO YOU HAVE AN APPROVED BUDGET SET UP FOR CREATING CONTENT (VIDEOS, PHOTOGRAPHY, PROPS) FOR THE PROFILES?	☐	☐
06	HAVE YOU SET ASIDE TIME IN YOUR MONTHLY SCHEDULE TO PLAN YOUR CONTENT AND GOALS?	☐	☐
07	HAVE YOU SET ASIDE TIME IN YOUR MONTHLY SCHEDULE FOR LEARNING AND DEVELOPMENT?	☐	☐
08	DO YOU HAVE CONTENT SCHEDULED ON A CALENDAR WITH A LIST OF WHAT YOU NEED TO POST THE CONTENT?	☐	☐

BRAINSTORMING

BRAINSTORMING CAN IDENTIFY WHAT IS HELPING OR STOPPING YOU FROM ACHIEVING YOUR GOALS. USE THE FOLLOWING SPACES TO BRAINSTORM TO SET YOURSELF UP FOR SUCCESS IN YOUR SOCIAL MEDIA MARKETING.

MY OVERALL GOALS FOR SOCIAL MEDIA THIS YEAR:

DEFINE SOCIAL MEDIA SUCCESS

WHAT DO YOU NEED TO DO NOW?

WHAT DO YOU NEED TO CHANGE?

WHAT TOOLS WILL YOU USE?

WHO WILL YOU ASK FOR HELP?

DEFINE YOUR GOALS

WRITE THREE MINI GOALS THAT CAN HELP YOU MEET YOUR OVERALL YOUR SOCIAL MEDIA MARKETING GOAL FOR THE YEAR. BE SURE TO THINK ABOUT WHAT GOALS ARE SUSTAINABLE AND HOW YOU'LL MEASURE THEM!

MY OVERALL GOAL FOR SOCIAL MEDIA THIS YEAR:

01

MINI GOAL ONE (THAT GETS ME CLOSER MY OVERALL GOAL)

_____

_____

_____

02

MINI GOAL TWO (THAT GETS ME CLOSER MY OVERALL GOAL)

_____

_____

_____

03

MINI GOAL THREE (THAT GETS ME CLOSER MY OVERALL GOAL)

_____

_____

_____

MY AUDIENCE

READ THE PROMTS BELOW AND WRITE DOWN THE FIRST THING THAT COMES TO MIND WHEN YOU THINK ABOUT YOUR AUDIENCE. FILL YOUR ANSWERS OUT IN THE BLANK BOXES. THIS WILL HELP YOU DETERMINE YOUR CONTENT.

MY AUDIENCE (POTENTIAL AND CURRENT CUSTOMERS) ARE PEOPLE WHO...

LOVE	
WANT TO	
ARE DRIVEN BY	
ARE INSPIRED BY	
HAVE A HABIT OF	
ARE HAPPIEST WHEN	
BELIEVE IN	
WOULD GIVE	
WILL ONE DAY	
HAVE THE GOAL OF	
NOTICE	
ARE AFRAID OF	

TOP 10

WRITE AND RANK THE TOP 10 MOST IMPORTANT THINGS YOU WANT YOUR
AUDIENCE TO KNOW WHEN THEY VISIT YOUR SOCIAL MEDIA PAGES.

	MOST IMPORTANT THINGS FOR MY AUDIENCE (CUSTOMERS) TO KNOW ABOUT ME, MY BUSINESS, OR MY ORGANIZATION:
01	
02	
03	
04	
05	
06	
07	
08	
09	
10	

PASSWORD TRACKER

Website/platform:

Username:

Password:

Email:

People with Access:

Website/platform:

Username:

Password:

Email:

People with Access:

Website/platform:

Username:

Password:

Email:

People with Access:

Website/platform:

Username:

Password:

Email:

People with Access:

Website/platform:

Username:

Password:

Email:

People with Access:

Website/platform:

Username:

Password:

Email:

People with Access:

SOCIAL MEDIA POST IDEAS - PART 1

The following are a mix of ideas for businesses, organizations, personal brands, and influencers. Circle the ones that work best for you or your brand and that you would enjoy creating.

countdown to the release of a new product or service	create an unboxing video of your latest product	share an exciting opt-in so people subscribe to your email list	share a video of your favorite product	share a quote to live by this week
inspire your audience to be brave today	share an event you will attend or sell at in your community	ask your audience what they would like to learn from you	reflect on the year & talk about future goals	write about the solutions your business has for a problem
educate your audience on your specific area of work	show growth by comparing past to present in your business/life	share a picture or video from your customers	share something that your audience would never believe	talk about the top 4 qualities of your product or service
share what your audience relates to about a problem you solve	talk about your favorite aspects of your product or service	talk about how your business or organization gives back	share an industry news source that interests you	create a would you rather do this or that post
share 3 words you want to reflect on and use this month	create a 3-day tip series for your audience in your niche	share a good review you received from a customer	give 5 top tips related to your industry	share your top 3 products or services and how they help people
share an event that is coming up	talk about the importance of your online community	show of your products or results of your service in a video	share a tip that you're loving right now	share your latest email newsletter

SOCIAL MEDIA POST IDEAS - PART 2

The following are a mix of ideas for businesses, organizations, personal brands, and influencers. Circle the ones that work best for you or your brand and that you would enjoy creating.

ask your audience a fun question	share what you do best with your audience	share 3 things on your bucket list	share a "behind the scenes" photo or video of your business	share your mission statement
inspire your audience to be kind today	create a video on the great things that happened this month	give your audience advice they can use today in your niche	create a video teaching something to your audience	share what you are grateful for and why
answer an FAQ that your audience might have	share someone else's post that inspires you	share a leap of faith you recently took in your life or business	share your goals for the year	talk about your business resolutions
talk about your main inspiration	share a picture of your office space	share a happy customer review	say happy birthday to your employee (be sure to include everyone)	share your top tips for using your product or service
post your top 4 selling products or services of the month	create an employee spotlight - what do they do everyday	share 9 facts about you to all your new followers	give 5 top tips related to your industry	share how you love to spend a Sunday afternoon
share your work routine	share industry specific advice with your audience	invite a special guest to talk about your industry or niche	share information about a community service event you sponsor	create a customer spotlight - how do they use your product or service

SOCIAL MEDIA POST IDEAS - PART 3

The following are a mix of ideas for businesses, organizations, personal brands, and influencers. Circle the ones that work best for you or your brand and that you would enjoy creating.

talk about your favorite book or resource	encourage your customers to share photos in return for freebies	share a milestone you recently reached in your business	share affirmations that you're loving this week	create a video using a new filter or music
create a challenge for your audience for the week	share something you are feeling thankful for today	share your to-do list for the day and ask your audience to share theirs	share something that makes you smile	write about your customers and why you love them
create a holiday post	share your latest case study	talk about how a client used your product or service in a new way	create a video with 7 tips related to your niche	reintroduce yourself in a video with currently trending audio
create a post that gives your audience 3-tips related to your niche	share 5 ways you can use your product or service	spotlight a regular customer	talk about your favorite thing to do during the holidays	share a blog you recently read and your thoughts about it
share a free resource with your audience	use a poll to learn more about your audience	create a video that is part of a challenge in your community	show behind the scenes of creating a video or a photo shoot	share the options you give people for products or services
shout-out and tag 3 accounts you love	share what you or your business values	share your process or work routine	share a sale or promo code	ask your audience what they would like to see more of from you

CHECKLIST FOR DESIGNING POSTS

☐ Write posts ahead of time, include key information, words, hashtags, and a call to action.

☐ Avoid using text in your pictures if possible. If you must use text, only use up to 2 different fonts.

☐ Ensure your post is to the point and easy to read. Read it out loud first. If you struggle with any of the words, rewrite the post.

☐ Include accessibility descriptions for photos and videos when required.

☐ Calls to action should include instructions for what the audience should do next: click here, visit us in store, double tap to love, shop now, sign up via the link in the bio.

☐ Ensure that photos are not blurry and are high resolution if possible.

☐ Script your videos ahead of time. Be sure they are clear, quick, and have a message with a call to action.

☐ Check for consistent branding on all your posts: i.e. you use the same tone of voice, logos, types of pictures etc.

☐ Consider using filters, music, and other options the platforms offer if this fits with what your audience would enjoy and is in line with your company/organization's policies, procedures, and branding.

Add additional checklist points that you want to be sure to fulfill here:

☐ _____

☐ _____

☐ _____

DIFFERENT TAGS EXPLAINED

Location Tags

Location tags connect your location with your photos and videos. This can be helpful if you are a business and you want people in your area to find you on social media. Take caution if you are an influencer without a storefront. Consider using a general location, like a general large city or area, to protect your privacy.

Tagging Profiles (@)

Tagging profiles can associate your business with other businesses and organizations that you partner with in your social media. This can be a helpful way for you and others to find new followers when promoting your products or services.

Hashtags (#)

Hashtags are still used on platforms to group together content for your audience to find. Do not use spaces in your tag. You can create a hashtag specific to your business or try out the following tags:

+ **Hashtags that help your audience find your product or service.**
   #headbands, #hostessgift, #businesscoach, #financialplan

+ **Hashtags that explain your niche.**
   #nutritioncoach #stockphotographer #marketingspecialist

+ **Hashtags that place you in communities in your specific niche.**
   #ebayseller #amazonfinds #entreprenuersupport #smallbusinessowners

+ **Hashtags that categorize your products or services during special events or holidays.**
   #valentinesday #blackfridaysale #holidayoutfit #christmasvibes

+ **Hashtags that show your location or where you sell online.**
   #smallbusinessalabama #Etsyshop #ClevelandPhotographer

+ **Hashtags that are allocated to a specific day.**
   #motivationalmonday #throwbackthursday #Fridayfeeling

COMMENTS

FOLLOWERS WILL COMMENT ON YOUR POSTS AND IT'S BEST TO HAVE A PLAN FOR TYPICAL QUESTIONS AND RESPONSES. USE THE BLANKS TO WRITE IN THE QUESTIONS YOU SEE MOST OFTEN ON YOUR POSTS AND BRAINSTORM YOUR ANSWERS. YOU CAN USE A VERSION OF THESE ANSWERS EVERY TIME TO RESPOND!

WHERE CAN I BUY THIS?	
WILL YOU RESTOCK THIS ITEM?	
WHAT SERVICES DO YOU OFFER?	

TURNING NEGATIVES INTO POSITIVES

WHAT SHOULD YOU DO ABOUT NEGATIVE COMMENTS? SOMETIMES FOLLOWERS AREN'T POSITIVE. THERE ARE FOUR OPTIONS: ANSWER IT, IGNORE IT, BLOCK IT, REPORT IT. MOST IMPORTANTLY, YOU HAVE CHOICES AND YOU ARE IN CONTROL OF YOUR ACCOUNT.

IN WHAT INSTANCES WILL YOU...

Answer It:

_____

_____

_____

_____

Ignore It:

_____

_____

_____

_____

Block It:

_____

_____

_____

_____

Report It:

_____

_____

_____

_____

BE SURE YOU COMPLETE THE FOLLOWING:

☐ Check the comments on your posts at least 1-3 times per week

☐ Check reviews on all platforms to ensure they are from legitimate customers

☐ Create a customer service plan so that if someone has a negative comment or review you can respond on the post with your concern, make suggestions on how you will fix the problem, and give the customer a way to contact you through direct messages or email. This shows everyone on the platform that you will give customers attention and solve any problems that may come up. This turns a negative into a positive.

SOCIAL MEDIA YEARLY PRIORITY MATRIX

LIST ALL THE SOCIAL MEDIA MARKETING TASKS YOU WANT TO COMPLETE THIS YEAR IN THE PRIORITY MATRIX. THIS WILL HELP YOU DETERMINE WHAT NEEDS TO BE DONE NOW AND HOW TO BALANCE YOUR SOCIAL MEDIA MARKETING ACTIONS.

	DO NOW	DO LATER
IMPORTANT	**GET IT DONE** (Important & urgent)	**SCHEDULE IT** (Important - not urgent)
NOT IMPORTANT	**DELEGATE IT** (Who else can do it)	**ELIMINATE IT** (not important, not urgent - delete)

YEARLY PRIORITY LIST

BASED ON YOUR PRIORITY MATRIX WHAT TASKS ARE HIGH VS LOW
PRIORITY FOR YOUR SOCIAL MEDIA MARKETING THIS YEAR?

HIGH PRIORITY

○ _____
○ _____
○ _____
○ _____
○ _____
○ _____
○ _____
○ _____

LOW PRIORITY

○ _____
○ _____
○ _____
○ _____
○ _____
○ _____
○ _____
○ _____

NOTES

PLATFORM PLANNER

checklists, to-do's, content, and tracking

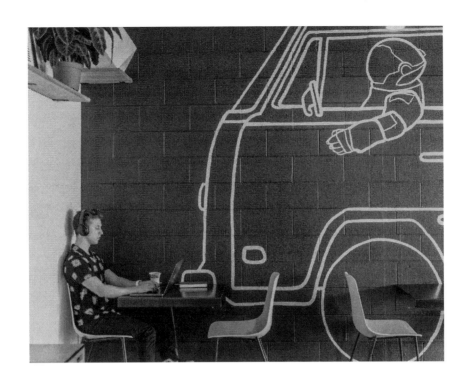

Make Your Social Media Work for You

Before starting this section repeat to yourself: "I do not need to be on every social media platform. I will only use the social media platforms that my customers use." Before you start planning your social media profiles, stop and take a look at your notes from the last section about your audience members. Your audience (i.e. your customers) probably are not on every platform. So you shouldn't be either! Choose 1-3 platforms in this workbook, and become very confident in using these platforms, then grow your outreach as you realize your customers are on other platforms. You can often reuse content across platforms, but for now focus on the basics to feel less stress and set yourself up for success.

FACEBOOK

FACEBOOK CHECKLIST

The following checklist can help you determine what you have already done with this social media platform and what to add to your to-do list for the future.

Page Set Up

☐ Select business/brand page or community/public figure

☐ Use a page name that is the same as your business name

☐ Include a correct business address and your business hours

☐ Set up page roles and fill with current employees

☐ Set up Meta business manager to advertise in the future

☐ Review Meta Business Suite

☐ Use a relevant image: either yourself or a logo as your profile picture

☐ Check multiple devices to make sure your Facebook cover photo is the correct size

☐ Cover photo caption includes call-to-action and links to your website

☐ Fill in your about section and include your website link

☐ Complete contact information especially if you have a location address with specific hours and a telephone number

Content

☐ Schedule regular posts, mulitiple times a week depending on your audience and content

☐ Showcase the best features of your products and services in content

☐ Use video as well as photos when creating content

☐ Ensure images are high-quality and not blurry

☐ Use templates on Canva and other applications to help you make content

☐ Include clear written call-to-actions in all content

☐ Check that content is engaging and speaks to what your audience wants

☐ Plan all your content in advance so you have time to make additional content as needed

☐ Track results from content with analytics

FACEBOOK CHECKLIST

The following checklist can help you determine what you have already done with this social media platform and what to add to your to-do list for the future.

Selling and Ads

☐ Complete research to determine ideal clients and best advertising types to reach them

☐ Ensure that your Facebook ads are on-brand with your business

☐ Check that the links for your website work before launching your ads and posts

☐ When posting about a specific product be sure you link the specific product to the post

☐ Track ad performance with analytics

☐ Create A/B tests to determine what gives you the best results

☐ Develop a clear understanding of Facebook ad rules and ensure your employees are aware of these rules

Extras

☐ Create a folder of edited photos that you can use anytime to create content

☐ Consult AI chat bots such as ChatGPT for extra ideas for content

☐ Create automated responses for Messenger

☐ Decide if you want to use online shops through Facebook as part of your selling strategy

☐ Prepare ahead of time to add AI to your pages as Meta offers these options in the future

☐ Create a VIP customer group for your followers and offer live sales with Comment Sold

☐ Create a group chat in Messenger for your followers

FACEBOOK TO-DO LIST

Daily

Post content according to your goals & schedule ☐

Share your content to one relevant group or page ☐

Engage in local or niche related groups ☐

Share your content to your stories ☐

Respond to any messages, comments & mentions ☐

Weekly

Review analytics for the week ☐

Join or follow 1-2 relevant groups or pages as you find them ☐

Check content for the coming week and add more to fix anything ahead of time ☐

Have a call-to-action for your audience for the week and promote it ☐

Check progress towards your goals ☐

Monthly

Review ads and sponsored posts results ☐

Set content & Facebook goals ☐

Check what worked & what didn't work the previous month ☐

Complete a review on what your current competitors are posting ☐

Reach out to any relevant sponsors, collaborators etc. for future content ☐

FACEBOOK CONTENT PLANNER

M

TIME	TYPE OF POST	TITLE	CONTENT NEEDED

T

TIME	TYPE OF POST	TITLE	CONTENT NEEDED

W

TIME	TYPE OF POST	TITLE	CONTENT NEEDED

T

TIME	TYPE OF POST	TITLE	CONTENT NEEDED

F

TIME	TYPE OF POST	TITLE	CONTENT NEEDED

S

TIME	TYPE OF POST	TITLE	CONTENT NEEDED

S

TIME	TYPE OF POST	TITLE	CONTENT NEEDED

FACEBOOK STATS BY MONTH

The following chart can help you track your stats over time to access data quickly and easily for reporting. You can find this information on the analytics pages of your social media platforms.

MONTH	TOTAL REACH	LIKES/FOLLOWS/ GROUP MEMBERS	ENGAGEMENT
JANUARY			
FEBRUARY			
MARCH			
APRIL			
MAY			
JUNE			
JULY			
AUGUST			
SEPTEMBER			
OCTOBER			
NOVEMBER			
DECEMBER			

FACEBOOK FOLLOWER TRACKER

Date reached:
_____

100

Date reached:
_____

200

Date reached:
_____

300

Date reached:
_____

400

Date reached:
_____

500

Date reached:
_____

1000

Date reached:
_____

1500

Date reached:
_____

2000

Date reached:
_____

2500

Date reached:
_____

3000

Date reached:
_____

3500

Date reached:
_____

4000

Date reached:
_____

4500

Date reached:
_____

5000

Date reached:
_____

5500

Date reached:
_____

6000

Date reached:
_____

7000

Date reached:
_____

8000

Date reached:
_____

9000

Date reached:
_____

10k!

ROI TRACKER

WRITE YOUR GOALS AND THE MEASUREMENTS YOU USED TO TRACK YOUR PROGRESS FROM YOUR ANALYTICS. USE THIS CHART TO DETERMINE WHAT YOU ARE DOING WELL AND WHERE YOU NEED TO REFOCUS YOUR EFFORTS.

YOUR GOAL AND MEASUREMENT FOR THE GOAL	DID YOU MEET THE GOAL? WHY OR WHY NOT?	WHAT ARE YOUR NEXT STEPS?

REFLECTION
Check In

✦ Your Wins

_____

_____

✦ Your Challenges

_____

_____

✦ How does it make you feel?

_____

_____

✦ How can you improve it?

_____

_____

What are four things you are excited to try next on this platform?

Reflections on what you learned:

_____

_____

_____

_____

INSTAGRAM

INSTAGRAM CHECKLIST

The following checklist can help you determine what you have already done with this social media platform and what to add to your to-do list for the future.

Profile Set Up

☐ Include your name and keywords in your Instagram bio for optimization purposes

☐ Ensure that your bio explains what your business or organization does

☐ Include updated ways to contact you (email, phone number, website)

☐ Include a branded hashtag if you want to use one

☐ Use a multi-link tool such as Linktree to add links to your bio

☐ Include a call-to-action in your bio

☐ Consider adding special characters, fonts, or emojis to attract attention

☐ Write your bio in a tone of voice that resonates with your audience include a lnk to your website or Linktree multi link tool

☐ Check that your username is easy to pronounce, spell, and find

☐ Be sure to relate your username to your business or organization name

☐ Leave out numbers and repetitive characters in your username

☐ Use a consistent profile picture across all social media platforms

☐ For a personal brand include a profile picture of you and for a non-personal brand include a logo that is easily recognizable

☐ Ensure that you or your logo stands out in your profile photo

INSTAGRAM CHECKLIST

The following checklist can help you determine what you have already done with this social media platform and what to add to your to-do list for the future.

Content

☐ Scroll through your feed and check if the purpose is clear to your audience

☐ Use a consistent tone of voice in all captions

☐ Use a consistent color theme and filter throughout your photos

☐ Post a mix of video and photo content

☐ Create calls to action on your post and include "link in the bio" in your caption

☐ Post to stories as well as your feed

☐ Create a schedule for Instagram lives, practice creating live posts on a private account just for your friends first

☐ Use trending audio, stickers, and filters in stories

☐ Encourage your audience to comment, double tap to heart, and engage with your content

☐ Use a mix of popular and personalized hashtags

☐ Tag your general location (such as city) if you have an in-person store, are posting travel photography, or promoting events in an area

☐ Stay consistent with where you post your hashtags: for example, always hide them in your comment section or always post them in the captions

Sales and Ads

☐ Review Meta for Business for sales and advertising options

☐ Decide if Instagram Shopping and Instagram Checkout should be part of your sales strategy

☐ Create branded content or partner with brands if it is part of your monetzation strategy

☐ Consider creating a broadcast channel if it meets your audience's interests

☐ Encourage followers to learn about and use badges when you go live

☐ Create exclusive content and experience through subscriptions

☐ Review Instagram Partner Monteization Policies and ensure your employees are aware of these too

INSTAGRAM TO-DO LIST

Daily

Post according to goals and schedule ☐

Engage with relevant niche related hashtags for 10 minutes ☐

Respond to any messages, mentions, shares etc. ☐

Engage on posts of people who follow you for 10-20 minutes ☐

Post to your stories ☐

Weekly

Review analytics for the week ☐

Ensure content is correct for the week to come ☐

Follow 5-10 people & engage with their accounts ☐

Have a call-to-action for your audience for the week and promote it ☐

Check progress towards monthly goals ☐

Monthly

Schedule content for the following month ☐

Set content and Instagram goals for the following month ☐

Check what worked and what didn't work the previous month ☐

Review what your current competitors are posting ☐

Reach out to any relevant sponsors, collaborators etc. ☐

INSTAGRAM CONTENT PLANNER

	TIME	TYPE OF POST	TITLE	CONTENT NEEDED
M				

	TIME	TYPE OF POST	TITLE	CONTENT NEEDED
T				

	TIME	TYPE OF POST	TITLE	CONTENT NEEDED
W				

	TIME	TYPE OF POST	TITLE	CONTENT NEEDED
T				

	TIME	TYPE OF POST	TITLE	CONTENT NEEDED
F				

	TIME	TYPE OF POST	TITLE	CONTENT NEEDED
S				

	TIME	TYPE OF POST	TITLE	CONTENT NEEDED
S				

INSTAGRAM STATS BY MONTH

The following chart can help you track your stats over time to access data quickly and easily for reporting. You can find this information on the analytics pages of your social media platforms.

MONTH	TOTAL REACH	LIKES/FOLLOWS/ GROUP MEMBERS	ENGAGEMENT
JANUARY			
FEBRUARY			
MARCH			
APRIL			
MAY			
JUNE			
JULY			
AUGUST			
SEPTEMBER			
OCTOBER			
NOVEMBER			
DECEMBER			

FOLLOWER TRACKER

Date reached:
_____

100

Date reached:
_____

200

Date reached:
_____

300

Date reached:
_____

400

Date reached:
_____

500

Date reached:
_____

1000

Date reached:
_____

1500

Date reached:
_____

2000

Date reached:
_____

2500

Date reached:
_____

3000

Date reached:
_____

3500

Date reached:
_____

4000

Date reached:
_____

4500

Date reached:
_____

5000

Date reached:
_____

5500

Date reached:
_____

6000

Date reached:
_____

7000

Date reached:
_____

8000

Date reached:
_____

9000

Date reached:
_____

10k!

ROI TRACKER

WRITE YOUR GOALS AND THE MEASUREMENTS YOU USED TO TRACK YOUR PROGRESS FROM YOUR ANALYTICS. USE THIS CHART TO DETERMINE WHAT YOU ARE DOING WELL AND WHERE YOU NEED TO REFOCUS YOUR EFFORTS.

YOUR GOAL AND MEASUREMENT FOR THE GOAL	DID YOU MEET THE GOAL? WHY OR WHY NOT?	WHAT ARE YOUR NEXT STEPS?

REFLECTION
Check In

✦ Your Wins

_____

_____

✦ Your Challenges

_____

_____

✦ How does it make you feel?

_____

_____

✦ How can you improve it?

_____

_____

What are four things you are excited to try next on this platform?

Reflections on what you learned:

_____

_____

_____

_____

LINKEDIN

LINKEDIN CHECKLIST

The following checklist can help you determine what you have already done with this social media platform and what to add to your to-do list for the future.

Profile Set Up

☐ Upload a professional on-brand profile image

☐ Add an on-brand background image

☐ Create a headline that contains relevant keywords

☐ Ensure that your headline clearly tells your audience what you do

☐ For personal profiles write a summary that clearly outlines your goals and achievements

☐ Include keywords in your summary and in your resume

☐ Ensure contact information is current

☐ Add your skills in order of importance

☐ Write and request endorsements and recommendations

☐ Add applicable certifications and your educational background so you can be found on alumni networks

☐ Review your sharing and public settings

Content & engagement

☐ Ensure content that you write yourself or share is relevant to your niche

☐ Ask thoughtful and insightful questions on your connections's posts

☐ Join or create groups relevant to your indusry, educational background, or interests

☐ Participate in groups and connect with others regularly

B2B Sales and Ads

☐ Decide if LinkedIn Marketing Solutions should be part of your ad strategy

☐ Boost content with native ads and sponsored posts that appear on LinkedIn

☐ Develop your business page and use showcase pages for specific brands or iniatives

☐ Publish industry specific articles and newsletters for your followers

☐ Review analytics on all advertisements and posts to check for engagement

LINKEDIN TO-DO LIST

Daily

Share your professional news and accomplishments ☐

Accept new connection requests and respond to messages ☐

Check notifications and messages ☐

Comment on relevant articles ☐

Spend a few minutes engaging with relevant hashtags ☐

Weekly

Reach out to new connections ☐

Leave recommendations or endorsements ☐

Publish a LinkedIn article ☐

Follow 3-5 new connections, accounts, and/or groups ☐

Check engagement for the week ☐

Monthly

Organize content for the month ☐

Add any new information to your profile ☐

Engage with your connections ☐

Check stats and analytics for the month ☐

Look at who viewed your profile and connect if desired ☐

LINKEDIN CONTENT PLANNER

M

TIME	TYPE OF POST	TITLE	CONTENT NEEDED

T

TIME	TYPE OF POST	TITLE	CONTENT NEEDED

W

TIME	TYPE OF POST	TITLE	CONTENT NEEDED

T

TIME	TYPE OF POST	TITLE	CONTENT NEEDED

F

TIME	TYPE OF POST	TITLE	CONTENT NEEDED

S

TIME	TYPE OF POST	TITLE	CONTENT NEEDED

S

TIME	TYPE OF POST	TITLE	CONTENT NEEDED

LINKEDIN STATS BY MONTH

The following chart can help you track your stats over time to access data quickly and easily for reporting. You can find this information on the analytics pages of your social media platforms.

MONTH	TOTAL REACH	LIKES/FOLLOWS/ GROUP MEMBERS	ENGAGEMENT
JANUARY			
FEBRUARY			
MARCH			
APRIL			
MAY			
JUNE			
JULY			
AUGUST			
SEPTEMBER			
OCTOBER			
NOVEMBER			
DECEMBER			

FOLLOWER TRACKER

Date reached: _____

Date reached: _____

Date reached: _____

Date reached: _____

Date reached: _____

100

200

300

400

500

Date reached: _____

Date reached: _____

Date reached: _____

Date reached: _____

Date reached: _____

1000

1500

2000

2500

3000

Date reached: _____

Date reached: _____

Date reached: _____

Date reached: _____

Date reached: _____

3500

4000

4500

5000

5500

Date reached: _____

Date reached: _____

Date reached: _____

Date reached: _____

Date reached: _____

6000

7000

8000

9000

10k!

ROI TRACKER

WRITE YOUR GOALS AND THE MEASUREMENTS YOU USED TO TRACK YOUR PROGRESS FROM YOUR ANALYTICS. USE THIS CHART TO DETERMINE WHAT YOU ARE DOING WELL AND WHERE YOU NEED TO REFOCUS YOUR EFFORTS.

YOUR GOAL AND MEASUREMENT FOR THE GOAL	DID YOU MEET THE GOAL? WHY OR WHY NOT?	WHAT ARE YOUR NEXT STEPS?

REFLECTION

Check In

✦ Your Wins

_____

_____

✦ Your Challenges

_____

_____

✦ How does it make you feel?

_____

_____

✦ How can you improve it?

_____

_____

What are four things you are excited to try next on this platform?

Reflections on what you learned:

_____

_____

_____

_____

PINTEREST

PINTEREST CHECKLIST

The following checklist can help you determine what you have already done with this social media platform and what to add to your to-do list for the future.

Profile Set Up

☐ Start a Pinterest Business account

☐ Ensure that your Pinterest username is consistent across social media platforms

☐ Enable rich pins (this pin syncs information from your website to the pin)

☐ Add your website address to your profile

☐ Create featured boards on your profile

☐ Make sure your profile picture for a personal brand is you or for a non-personal brand is your logo

☐ Include your business name, information, keywords, and a call to action in your bio

Boards and Pins

☐ Develop a branded board for your own content that links to your website

☐ Set up a board for other people's content that your audience will find useful

☐ Delete or hide all personal or irrelevant boards

☐ Develop at least 5 boards with at least 35 pins related to the board title

☐ Create pins that link to products and services on your website

☐ Review Pinterest for Creators to use the most current content tools

☐ Ensure all pins are vertical graphics or video

☐ Use easy to read, short text on pins

☐ Use music, stickers, voice over, and other effects on pins

☐ Encourage your audience to save your content in the pin itself or caption

☐ Use tags (up to 10) for all pins

☐ Add collaborators on group boards for brand and influencer partnerships

PINTEREST CHECKLIST

The following checklist can help you determine what you have already done with this social media platform and what to add to your to-do list for the future.

Selling and Ads

☐ Create a Pinterest Ads Manager account

☐ Review analytics to ensure engagement

☐ Use automated targets and actalikes on Pinterest to find your audience

☐ Make your pins shopable

☐ Tag pins with affliate links when it makes sense for your selling strategy

☐ Develop paid partnerships with brands

☐ Review Pinterest Ads Manager

Extras

☐ Use Pinterest Predicts and Trends Tools to see upcoming trends you can use yourself

☐ Review the Pinterest Creator Code and ensure that your employees follow this

☐ Work with AR (augmented reality) tools to let your audience virtually try-on products

☐ Consider using Pinterest Catalogues to place your products for sale online

PINTEREST TO-DO LIST

Daily

Pin 10-30 old pins to relevant boards ☐

Follow 5 relevant pinners ☐

Add 3-5 new pins ☐

Repin 10-20 pins (from other accounts) ☐

Weekly

Review analytics for the week ☐

Join 2 new group boards ☐

Comment on 10-15 other pins ☐

Share Pinterest links to social media sites ☐

Take time to start designing new pins ☐

Monthly

Schedule pins that are both video and photos ☐

Create pins for the entire month ☐

Check on Pinterest Trends and use upcoming trends in your content ☐

Review your most popular pins for the last 30 days ☐

PINTEREST EVERYDAY CONTENT PLANNER

	TIME	TYPE OF POST	TITLE	CONTENT NEEDED
M				

	TIME	TYPE OF POST	TITLE	CONTENT NEEDED
T				

	TIME	TYPE OF POST	TITLE	CONTENT NEEDED
W				

	TIME	TYPE OF POST	TITLE	CONTENT NEEDED
T				

	TIME	TYPE OF POST	TITLE	CONTENT NEEDED
F				

	TIME	TYPE OF POST	TITLE	CONTENT NEEDED
S				

	TIME	TYPE OF POST	TITLE	CONTENT NEEDED
S				

PINTEREST STATS BY MONTH

The following chart can help you track your stats over time to access data quickly and easily for reporting. You can find this information on the analytics pages of your social media platforms.

MONTH	TOTAL REACH	LIKES/FOLLOWS/ GROUP MEMBERS	ENGAGEMENT
JANUARY			
FEBRUARY			
MARCH			
APRIL			
MAY			
JUNE			
JULY			
AUGUST			
SEPTEMBER			
OCTOBER			
NOVEMBER			
DECEMBER			

FOLLOWER TRACKER

Date reached:
_____

100

Date reached:
_____

200

Date reached:
_____

300

Date reached:
_____

400

Date reached:
_____

500

Date reached:
_____

1000

Date reached:
_____

1500

Date reached:
_____

2000

Date reached:
_____

2500

Date reached:
_____

3000

Date reached:
_____

3500

Date reached:
_____

4000

Date reached:
_____

4500

Date reached:
_____

5000

Date reached:
_____

5500

Date reached:
_____

6000

Date reached:
_____

7000

Date reached:
_____

8000

Date reached:
_____

9000

Date reached:
_____

10k!

ROI TRACKER

WRITE YOUR GOALS AND THE MEASUREMENTS YOU USED TO TRACK YOUR PROGRESS FROM YOUR ANALYTICS. USE THIS CHART TO DETERMINE WHAT YOU ARE DOING WELL AND WHERE YOU NEED TO REFOCUS YOUR EFFORTS.

YOUR GOAL AND MEASUREMENT FOR THE GOAL	DID YOU MEET THE GOAL? WHY OR WHY NOT?	WHAT ARE YOUR NEXT STEPS?

REFLECTION

✦ Your Wins

_____

_____

✦ Your Challenges

_____

_____

✦ How does it make you feel?

_____

_____

✦ How can you improve it?

_____

_____

What are four things you are excited to try next on this platform?

Reflections on what you learned:

_____

_____

_____

_____

TIKTOK

TIKTOK CHECKLIST

The following checklist can help you determine what you have already done with this social media platform and what to add to your to-do list for the future.

Profile Set Up

☐ Create a username that is your business name or relates to what you do

☐ Use a profile image that is easily identifiable

☐ Review the differences between a business and personal account and choose the one that works best for you and your goals

☐ Include info about your account and what you'll bring to the community in your bio

☐ Decide what your videos will do - are they entertaining, educating, and/or impactful?

☐ Complete the business registration for an official business account

☐ See the Business Creative Hub for more inspiration for your profile

☐ Use the auto-message option to write a preset response for direct messages

Videos

☐ Use the TikTok Creative Center to see trending hashtags and content

☐ Plan your videos: consider who will be in the videos, music, filters, and theme

☐ Practice creating TikTok videos with different effects to see what you like best

☐ Write captions that include a call to action and encourage audience engagement

☐ Use the Discover page (the magnifying glass) to research different videos

☐ Set up your lighting with windows, lamps, a light tripod, or even Christmas lights

☐ Shoot your video vertically to take up the most screen space.

☐ Support your phone with a stand, or set it up against books or other objects

Selling and Ads

☐ Review in-feed ads and create an Ads Manager account

☐ Use TikTok Creator Marketplace to find creator partners or become a creator

☐ Create video shopping ads and a TikTok shop to sell directly to your audience

☐ Measure your progress with analytics

TIKTOK TO-DO LIST

Daily

Research trending TikTok songs, dances, and other content ☐

Review video content you want to use now or later in future posts ☐

Experiment with different effects, songs, sound, and features ☐

Heart (like) 5-10 videos in your industry or niche area ☐

Lean into the TikTok community by actively engaging in your feed ☐

Weekly

Upload 2-3 videos each week ☐

Stay consistent in your video's formatting, production, and style ☐

Comment on 10 other videos in your industry or niche area ☐

Credit originators of trends, dances, or other trends ☐

Include accessibility options such as autocaptions and text to speech ☐

Monthly

Plan to participate in 2-3 creative challenges and trends each month ☐

Review updates to community guidelines, features, and new opportunities ☐

Check over your profile and ensure keywords are relevant ☐

Check analytics on your most popular videos for the last 30 days ☐

TIKTOK EVERYDAY CONTENT PLANNER

	TIME	TYPE OF POST	TITLE	CONTENT NEEDED
M				

	TIME	TYPE OF POST	TITLE	CONTENT NEEDED
T				

	TIME	TYPE OF POST	TITLE	CONTENT NEEDED
W				

	TIME	TYPE OF POST	TITLE	CONTENT NEEDED
T				

	TIME	TYPE OF POST	TITLE	CONTENT NEEDED
F				

	TIME	TYPE OF POST	TITLE	CONTENT NEEDED
S				

	TIME	TYPE OF POST	TITLE	CONTENT NEEDED
S				

TIKTOK STATS BY MONTH

The following chart can help you track your stats over time to access data quickly and easily for reporting. You can find this information on the analytics pages of your social media platforms.

MONTH	TOTAL REACH	LIKES/FOLLOWS/ GROUP MEMBERS	ENGAGEMENT
JANUARY			
FEBRUARY			
MARCH			
APRIL			
MAY			
JUNE			
JULY			
AUGUST			
SEPTEMBER			
OCTOBER			
NOVEMBER			
DECEMBER			

FOLLOWER TRACKER

Date reached: _____

Date reached: _____

Date reached: _____

Date reached: _____

Date reached: _____

100

200

300

400

500

Date reached: _____

Date reached: _____

Date reached: _____

Date reached: _____

Date reached: _____

1000

1500

2000

2500

3000

Date reached: _____

Date reached: _____

Date reached: _____

Date reached: _____

Date reached: _____

3500

4000

4500

5000

5500

Date reached: _____

Date reached: _____

Date reached: _____

Date reached: _____

Date reached: _____

6000

7000

8000

9000

10k!

ROI TRACKER

WRITE YOUR GOALS AND THE MEASUREMENTS YOU USED TO TRACK YOUR PROGRESS FROM YOUR ANALYTICS. USE THIS CHART TO DETERMINE WHAT YOU ARE DOING WELL AND WHERE YOU NEED TO REFOCUS YOUR EFFORTS.

YOUR GOAL AND MEASUREMENT FOR THE GOAL	DID YOU MEET THE GOAL? WHY OR WHY NOT?	WHAT ARE YOUR NEXT STEPS?

REFLECTION

Check In

✦ Your Wins

_____

_____

✦ Your Challenges

_____

_____

✦ How does it make you feel?

_____

_____

✦ How can you improve it?

_____

_____

What are four things you are excited to try next on this platform?

Reflections on what you learned:

_____

_____

_____

_____

YOUTUBE

YOUTUBE CHECKLIST

The following checklist can help you determine what you have already done with this social media platform and what to add to your to-do list for the future.

Profile Set Up

☐ Ensure the name of your channel is relevant to business or personal brand

☐ Describe your channel clearly (what you are all about) in your profile

☐ Link your website to your channel

☐ Use a profile picture that is an image of you or logo

☐ Use a banner image that is on-brand and attention grabbing

☐ Ensure overall branding of channel is cohesive: brand voice, audience, and thumbnail images are consistent. Your overall YouTube branding matches website and social media pages too.

☐ Create organized and relevant playlists that match your audiences's interests

Videos

☐ Video file name uses optimized description

☐ Video title matches file name and uses keywords

☐ Video title accurately describes video

☐ Keywords used in your tags

☐ Thumbnail is on-brand, attention grabbing, and easy to understand

☐ Video description uses keywords and contains relevant links

☐ Video added to relevant playlists

☐ Video is added to the correct category

☐ Video uploaded during peak engagement time

☐ Social sharing; promote your videos on relevant social media platforms

☐ Call-to-actions; include call-to-actions in your videos such as "subscribe to our channel", "like this video", "click on the link in the description"

YOUTUBE CHECKLIST

The following checklist can help you determine what you have already done with this social media platform and what to add to your to-do list for the future.

Selling and Ads

☐ Choose an ad format for your video based on your goals

☐ Use the Find My Audience tool to discover new audiences

☐ Use YouTube video creation tools to develop content you already have into ads

☐ Measure your results with analytics

☐ Research other creators and success stories on YouTube Advertising

☐ Explore YouTube Shopping and decide if it should be part of your selling strategy

Extras

☐ Earn a Google Ads Video Certification

☐ Review the YouTube Ads Leaderboard to see the top ads people watch

☐ Research how AI will change the way YouTube content is made in the future

☐ For individuals, check out the YouTube Partner Program to monetize your profile

☐ Review YouTube Community Guidelines and ensure your employees know the rules

☐ Decide if channel memberships, Super Stickers, Super Thanks, and Super Chat should be part of your selling strategy

YOUTUBE TO-DO LIST

Daily

Respond to comments ☐

Like, share, or comment on relevant videos ☐

Check next video publishing date ☐

Make sure all video descriptions are up-to-date ☐

Work on content for your next video ☐

Weekly

Check stats for previous week ☐

Update profile if needed ☐

Confirm video schedule for the week ☐

Proofread content for upcoming videos ☐

Create graphics ☐

Monthly

Organize content for the month ☐

Add any new info to profile (social links, side bar, banner etc.) ☐

Create content for the next month ☐

Check monthly stats ☐

Determine what worked well and what didn't and adjust strategy accordingly ☐

YOUTUBE EVERYDAY CONTENT PLANNER

M

TIME	TYPE OF POST	TITLE	CONTENT NEEDED

T

TIME	TYPE OF POST	TITLE	CONTENT NEEDED

W

TIME	TYPE OF POST	TITLE	CONTENT NEEDED

T

TIME	TYPE OF POST	TITLE	CONTENT NEEDED

F

TIME	TYPE OF POST	TITLE	CONTENT NEEDED

S

TIME	TYPE OF POST	TITLE	CONTENT NEEDED

S

TIME	TYPE OF POST	TITLE	CONTENT NEEDED

YOUTUBE STATS BY MONTH

The following chart can help you track your stats over time to access data quickly and easily for reporting. You can find this information on the analytics pages of your social media platforms.

MONTH	TOTAL REACH	LIKES/FOLLOWS/ GROUP MEMBERS	ENGAGEMENT
JANUARY			
FEBRUARY			
MARCH			
APRIL			
MAY			
JUNE			
JULY			
AUGUST			
SEPTEMBER			
OCTOBER			
NOVEMBER			
DECEMBER			

FOLLOWER TRACKER

Date reached:

_____

100

Date reached:

_____

200

Date reached:

_____

300

Date reached:

_____

400

Date reached:

_____

500

Date reached:

_____

1000

Date reached:

_____

1500

Date reached:

_____

2000

Date reached:

_____

2500

Date reached:

_____

3000

Date reached:

_____

3500

Date reached:

_____

4000

Date reached:

_____

4500

Date reached:

_____

5000

Date reached:

_____

5500

Date reached:

_____

6000

Date reached:

_____

7000

Date reached:

_____

8000

Date reached:

_____

9000

Date reached:

_____

10k!

ROI TRACKER

WRITE YOUR GOALS AND THE MEASUREMENTS YOU USED TO TRACK YOUR PROGRESS FROM YOUR ANALYTICS. USE THIS CHART TO DETERMINE WHAT YOU ARE DOING WELL AND WHERE YOU NEED TO REFOCUS YOUR EFFORTS.

YOUR GOAL AND MEASUREMENT FOR THE GOAL	DID YOU MEET THE GOAL? WHY OR WHY NOT?	WHAT ARE YOUR NEXT STEPS?

REFLECTION
Check In

✦ Your Wins

_____

_____

✦ Your Challenges

_____

_____

✦ How does it make you feel?

_____

_____

✦ How can you improve it?

_____

_____

What are four things you are excited to try next on this platform?

Reflections on what you learned:

_____

_____

_____

_____

THE STRESS LESS GUIDE

X
(FORMERLY KNOWN AS TWITTER)

X (TWITTER) CHECKLIST

The following checklist can help you determine what you have already done with this social media platform and what to add to your to-do list for the future.

Profile Set Up

☐ Choose a recognizable photo or your logo for your profile picture

☐ Ensure your header image is on-brand and showcases new launches or campaigns

☐ Chose a username (@_____) that is recognizable and tied to your business

☐ Use 160 characters in your bio to tell your audience what you do

☐ Link your website to your bio

Posts

☐ Ensure that your brand voice is consistent in your posts

☐ Pin a post to your profile that is your top news, an ongoing sale, or a product launch

☐ Make use a of a scheduler tool to save time

☐ Use keywords and hashtags to discuss trending topics

☐ Use 1-2 hashtags and keep posts short (280 characters)

☐ Link to relevant content and websites

☐ Post during peak times or events that you know your audience is watching

☐ Ensure your posts have clear calls to action

Selling and Ads

☐ Sign up for X Premium or Verified Organizations to run ads

☐ Use Flight School to learn more about ad content and creation

☐ Research different X products to create new features on your profile

☐ Review X Community Guidelines and ensure that your employees are aware of the rules

X (TWITTER) TO-DO LIST

Daily

Respond to posts ☐

Post according to your daily (1-2 times per day) goal ☐

Repost 3-5 posts by other X users ☐

Follow 3-5 new accounts ☐

Respond to any direct messages ☐

Weekly

Review analytics for the week ☐

Check hashtag performance ☐

Check content for the coming week ☐

Have a call to action for your audience for the week & promote it ☐

Check progress towards monthly goals ☐

Monthly

Schedule content for the following month ☐

Research new features and tools to determine if they are a fit for your profile ☐

Check what worked & what didn't work the previous month ☐

Review your current competitors's profiles ☐

Reach out to any relevant sponsors, collaborators etc. ☐

X (TWITTER) EVERYDAY CONTENT PLANNER

	TIME	TYPE OF POST	TITLE	CONTENT NEEDED
M				

	TIME	TYPE OF POST	TITLE	CONTENT NEEDED
T				

	TIME	TYPE OF POST	TITLE	CONTENT NEEDED
W				

	TIME	TYPE OF POST	TITLE	CONTENT NEEDED
T				

	TIME	TYPE OF POST	TITLE	CONTENT NEEDED
F				

	TIME	TYPE OF POST	TITLE	CONTENT NEEDED
S				

	TIME	TYPE OF POST	TITLE	CONTENT NEEDED
S				

X (TWITTER) STATS BY MONTH

The following chart can help you track your stats over time to access data quickly and easily for reporting. You can find this information on the analytics pages of your social media platforms.

MONTH	TOTAL REACH	LIKES/FOLLOWS/ GROUP MEMBERS	ENGAGEMENT
JANUARY			
FEBRUARY			
MARCH			
APRIL			
MAY			
JUNE			
JULY			
AUGUST			
SEPTEMBER			
OCTOBER			
NOVEMBER			
DECEMBER			

FOLLOWER TRACKER

Date reached:

_____

100

Date reached:

_____

200

Date reached:

_____

300

Date reached:

_____

400

Date reached:

_____

500

Date reached:

_____

1000

Date reached:

_____

1500

Date reached:

_____

2000

Date reached:

_____

2500

Date reached:

_____

3000

Date reached:

_____

3500

Date reached:

_____

4000

Date reached:

_____

4500

Date reached:

_____

5000

Date reached:

_____

5500

Date reached:

_____

6000

Date reached:

_____

7000

Date reached:

_____

8000

Date reached:

_____

9000

Date reached:

_____

10k!

ROI TRACKER

WRITE YOUR GOALS AND THE MEASUREMENTS YOU USED TO TRACK YOUR PROGRESS FROM YOUR ANALYTICS. USE THIS CHART TO DETERMINE WHAT YOU ARE DOING WELL AND WHERE YOU NEED TO REFOCUS YOUR EFFORTS.

YOUR GOAL AND MEASUREMENT FOR THE GOAL	DID YOU MEET THE GOAL? WHY OR WHY NOT?	WHAT ARE YOUR NEXT STEPS?

REFLECTION
Check In

✦ Your Wins

_____

_____

✦ Your Challenges

_____

_____

✦ How does it make you feel?

_____

_____

✦ How can you improve it?

_____

_____

What are four things you are excited to try next on this platform?

Reflections on what you learned:

_____

_____

_____

_____

FILL IN YOUR OWN PLATFORM

If you are using a platform not listed in this workbook, use these pages to create your own checklists and spaces for reflection.

_____ CHECKLIST

The following checklist can help you determine what you have already done with this social media platform and what to add to your to-do list for the future.

Profile Set Up

☐

☐

☐

☐

☐

Content

☐

☐

☐

☐

☐

☐

☐

☐

Selling and Ads

☐

☐

☐

☐

☐

_____ TO-DO LIST

Daily

☐
☐
☐
☐
☐

Weekly

☐
☐
☐
☐
☐

Monthly

☐
☐
☐
☐
☐

_____ EVERYDAY CONTENT PLANNER

TIME	TYPE OF POST	TITLE	CONTENT NEEDED

M

TIME	TYPE OF POST	TITLE	CONTENT NEEDED

T

TIME	TYPE OF POST	TITLE	CONTENT NEEDED

W

TIME	TYPE OF POST	TITLE	CONTENT NEEDED

T

TIME	TYPE OF POST	TITLE	CONTENT NEEDED

F

TIME	TYPE OF POST	TITLE	CONTENT NEEDED

S

TIME	TYPE OF POST	TITLE	CONTENT NEEDED

S

_____ STATS BY MONTH

The following chart can help you track your stats over time to access data quickly and easily for reporting. You can find this information on the analytics pages of your social media platforms.

MONTH	TOTAL REACH	LIKES/FOLLOWS/ GROUP MEMBERS	ENGAGEMENT
JANUARY			
FEBRUARY			
MARCH			
APRIL			
MAY			
JUNE			
JULY			
AUGUST			
SEPTEMBER			
OCTOBER			
NOVEMBER			
DECEMBER			

ROI TRACKER

WRITE YOUR GOALS AND THE MEASUREMENTS YOU USED TO TRACK YOUR PROGRESS FROM YOUR ANALYTICS. USE THIS CHART TO DETERMINE WHAT YOU ARE DOING WELL AND WHERE YOU NEED TO REFOCUS YOUR EFFORTS.

YOUR GOAL AND MEASUREMENT FOR THE GOAL	DID YOU MEET THE GOAL? WHY OR WHY NOT?	WHAT ARE YOUR NEXT STEPS?

REFLECTION
Check In

✦ Your Wins

_____

_____

✦ Your Challenges

_____

_____

✦ How does it make you feel?

_____

_____

✦ How can you improve it?

_____

_____

What are four things you are excited to try next on this platform?

Reflections on what you learned:

_____

_____

_____

_____

SOCIAL MEDIA CAMPAIGN PLANNER

tasks and milestones

Develop Campaigns to Meet Your Goals

Campaigns are overarching plans to meet your goals through social media. Develop campaigns that help you think about all the ways you can meet your goals and the various content (or individual videos, photos, text, and posts you will make on the social media platforms to get you past the finish line. For example, you have a new product or service launching this year. Your campaign will take place before the launch and will include an objective, i.e. let my audience members know about the new product or service and then all the tasks you need to complete to do this. Tasks might include taking photos of the new product or people using the service or asking early customers to write a review you can post. The appendix at the end of this workbook includes an example of a campaign planner. The following blank planner pages are here for your campaigns this year.

CAMPAIGN PLANNER

Tip: Feeling stuck?
Check the appendix
for an example!

START DATE

Objective of Campaign: The Goal You Will Reach & How

END DATE

Milestones to Make it Happen

Task	Assigned To	Done

Notes

CAMPAIGN PLANNER

START DATE

Objective of Campaign: The Goal You Will Reach & How

END DATE

Milestones to Make it Happen

_____

_____

_____

_____

Task	Assigned To	Done

Notes

CAMPAIGN PLANNER

START DATE

END DATE

Objective of Campaign: The Goal You Will Reach & How

Milestones to Make it Happen

_____

_____

_____

_____

Task	Assigned To	Done

Notes

CAMPAIGN PLANNER

START DATE

Objective of Campaign: The Goal You Will Reach & How

END DATE

Milestones to Make it Happen

_____

_____

_____

_____

Task	Assigned To	Done

Notes

CAMPAIGN PLANNER

START DATE

END DATE

Objective of Campaign: The Goal You Will Reach & How

Milestones to Make it Happen

_____

_____

_____

_____

Task	Assigned To	Done

Notes

CAMPAIGN PLANNER

START DATE

END DATE

Objective of Campaign: The Goal You Will Reach & How

Milestones to Make it Happen

_____

_____

_____

_____

Task	Assigned To	Done

Notes

CAMPAIGN PLANNER

START DATE

Objective of Campaign: The Goal You Will Reach & How

END DATE

Milestones to Make it Happen

_____

_____

_____

_____

Task	Assigned To	Done

Notes

MONTHLY CONTENT PLANNER

weekly

Lights, Camera, Action!

Content is made up of all the individual photographs, videos, text, blogs, websites, and anything you make to promote your product or service online. Making content can be overwhelming. Key decisions include who will be in the content, what the content will look like and banking enough content so you can pull from materials time and time again for multiple social media profiles. The appendix at the end of this workbook includes an example of a content planner. The following blank planner pages are for your content this year.

JANUARY CONTENT PLANNER

Tip: Feeling stuck? Check the appendix for an example!

MAIN FOCUS -

WEEK 1	WEEK 2

WEEK 3	WEEK 4

To-do list

- [ ] _____
- [ ] _____
- [ ] _____
- [ ] _____
- [ ] _____
- [ ] _____
- [ ] _____
- [ ] _____
- [ ] _____
- [ ] _____
- [ ] _____
- [ ] _____
- [ ] _____
- [ ] _____

Notes

FEBRUARY CONTENT PLANNER

MAIN FOCUS -

WEEK 1	WEEK 2

WEEK 3	WEEK 4

To-do list

_____ ☐

_____ ☐

_____ ☐

_____ ☐

_____ ☐

_____ ☐

_____ ☐

_____ ☐

_____ ☐

_____ ☐

_____ ☐

_____ ☐

_____ ☐

_____ ☐

_____ ☐

Notes

MARCH CONTENT PLANNER

MAIN FOCUS -

WEEK 1	WEEK 2

WEEK 3	WEEK 4

To-do list

- _____ ☐
- _____ ☐
- _____ ☐
- _____ ☐
- _____ ☐
- _____ ☐
- _____ ☐
- _____ ☐
- _____ ☐
- _____ ☐
- _____ ☐
- _____ ☐
- _____ ☐
- _____ ☐

Notes

APRIL CONTENT PLANNER

MAIN FOCUS -

WEEK 1	WEEK 2

To-do list

- [ ] _____
- [ ] _____
- [ ] _____
- [ ] _____
- [ ] _____
- [ ] _____
- [ ] _____
- [ ] _____
- [ ] _____
- [ ] _____
- [ ] _____
- [ ] _____
- [ ] _____
- [ ] _____
- [ ] _____

WEEK 3	WEEK 4

Notes

MAY CONTENT PLANNER

MAIN FOCUS -

WEEK 1	WEEK 2

To-do list

- [ ] _____
- [ ] _____
- [ ] _____
- [ ] _____
- [ ] _____
- [ ] _____
- [ ] _____
- [ ] _____

WEEK 3	WEEK 4

- [ ] _____
- [ ] _____
- [ ] _____
- [ ] _____
- [ ] _____
- [ ] _____

Notes

JUNE CONTENT PLANNER

MAIN FOCUS -

WEEK 1	WEEK 2

WEEK 3	WEEK 4

To-do list

- [ ] _____
- [ ] _____
- [ ] _____
- [ ] _____
- [ ] _____
- [ ] _____
- [ ] _____
- [ ] _____
- [ ] _____
- [ ] _____
- [ ] _____
- [ ] _____
- [ ] _____
- [ ] _____

Notes

JULY CONTENT PLANNER

MAIN FOCUS -

WEEK 1	WEEK 2

WEEK 3	WEEK 4

To-do list

- [ ] _____
- [ ] _____
- [ ] _____
- [ ] _____
- [ ] _____
- [ ] _____
- [ ] _____
- [ ] _____
- [ ] _____
- [ ] _____
- [ ] _____
- [ ] _____
- [ ] _____
- [ ] _____

Notes

AUGUST CONTENT PLANNER

MAIN FOCUS -

WEEK 1	WEEK 2

WEEK 3	WEEK 4

To-do list

- [ ] _____
- [ ] _____
- [ ] _____
- [ ] _____
- [ ] _____
- [ ] _____
- [ ] _____
- [ ] _____
- [ ] _____
- [ ] _____
- [ ] _____
- [ ] _____
- [ ] _____
- [ ] _____

Notes

SEPTEMBER CONTENT PLANNER

MAIN FOCUS -

WEEK 1	WEEK 2

WEEK 3	WEEK 4

To-do list

- [ ] _____
- [ ] _____
- [ ] _____
- [ ] _____
- [ ] _____
- [ ] _____
- [ ] _____
- [ ] _____
- [ ] _____
- [ ] _____
- [ ] _____
- [ ] _____
- [ ] _____
- [ ] _____

Notes

OCTOBER CONTENT PLANNER

MAIN FOCUS -

WEEK 1	WEEK 2

To-do list

- [ ] _____
- [ ] _____
- [ ] _____
- [ ] _____
- [ ] _____
- [ ] _____
- [ ] _____

WEEK 3	WEEK 4

- [ ] _____
- [ ] _____
- [ ] _____
- [ ] _____
- [ ] _____
- [ ] _____
- [ ] _____

Notes

NOVEMBER CONTENT PLANNER

MAIN FOCUS -

WEEK 1	WEEK 2

To-do list

- ☐
- ☐
- ☐
- ☐
- ☐
- ☐
- ☐
- ☐
- ☐
- ☐
- ☐
- ☐
- ☐
- ☐

WEEK 3	WEEK 4

Notes

DECEMBER CONTENT PLANNER

MAIN FOCUS -

WEEK 1	WEEK 2

To-do list

- [ ] _____
- [ ] _____
- [ ] _____
- [ ] _____
- [ ] _____
- [ ] _____
- [ ] _____

WEEK 3	WEEK 4

- [ ] _____
- [ ] _____
- [ ] _____
- [ ] _____
- [ ] _____
- [ ] _____
- [ ] _____

Notes

YEARLY CONTENT CALENDAR

undated

Let's Plan This Out in Advance

While some things may be changing constantly in social media marketing and your business, other things are not. Use this space to plan ahead for your business or organization's big dates, employee spotlights, product launches, and other opportunities. Did you know most major magazines create content 6-8 months in advance? Publishing companies create books 3-4 years in advance. You should create your work in advance too! This way you can go ahead and make content now for these events and only make content for surprise events and things you want to cover in the moment.

JANUARY CONTENT CALENDAR

Tip: Feeling stuck? Check the appendix for an example!

MONDAY	TUESDAY	WEDNESDAY	THURSDAY	FRIDAY	SATURDAY	SUNDAY
☐	☐	☐	☐	☐	☐	☐
☐	☐	☐	☐	☐	☐	☐
☐	☐	☐	☐	☐	☐	☐
☐	☐	☐	☐	☐	☐	☐
☐	☐	☐	☐	☐	☐	☐
☐	☐	☐	☐	☐	☐	☐

FEBRUARY CONTENT CALENDAR

MONDAY	TUESDAY	WEDNESDAY	THURSDAY	FRIDAY	SATURDAY	SUNDAY
☐	☐	☐	☐	☐	☐	☐
☐	☐	☐	☐	☐	☐	☐
☐	☐	☐	☐	☐	☐	☐
☐	☐	☐	☐	☐	☐	☐
☐	☐	☐	☐	☐	☐	☐
☐	☐	☐	☐	☐	☐	☐

MARCH CONTENT CALENDAR

MONDAY	TUESDAY	WEDNESDAY	THURSDAY	FRIDAY	SATURDAY	SUNDAY
☐	☐	☐	☐	☐	☐	☐
☐	☐	☐	☐	☐	☐	☐
☐	☐	☐	☐	☐	☐	☐
☐	☐	☐	☐	☐	☐	☐
☐	☐	☐	☐	☐	☐	☐
☐	☐	☐	☐	☐	☐	☐

APRIL CONTENT CALENDAR

MONDAY	TUESDAY	WEDNESDAY	THURSDAY	FRIDAY	SATURDAY	SUNDAY
☐	☐	☐	☐	☐	☐	☐
☐	☐	☐	☐	☐	☐	☐
☐	☐	☐	☐	☐	☐	☐
☐	☐	☐	☐	☐	☐	☐
☐	☐	☐	☐	☐	☐	☐
☐	☐	☐	☐	☐	☐	☐

MAY CONTENT CALENDAR

MONDAY	TUESDAY	WEDNESDAY	THURSDAY	FRIDAY	SATURDAY	SUNDAY
☐	☐	☐	☐	☐	☐	☐
☐	☐	☐	☐	☐	☐	☐
☐	☐	☐	☐	☐	☐	☐
☐	☐	☐	☐	☐	☐	☐
☐	☐	☐	☐	☐	☐	☐
☐	☐	☐	☐	☐	☐	☐

JUNE CONTENT CALENDAR

MONDAY	TUESDAY	WEDNESDAY	THURSDAY	FRIDAY	SATURDAY	SUNDAY
☐	☐	☐	☐	☐	☐	☐
☐	☐	☐	☐	☐	☐	☐
☐	☐	☐	☐	☐	☐	☐
☐	☐	☐	☐	☐	☐	☐
☐	☐	☐	☐	☐	☐	☐
☐	☐	☐	☐	☐	☐	☐

JULY CONTENT CALENDAR

MONDAY	TUESDAY	WEDNESDAY	THURSDAY	FRIDAY	SATURDAY	SUNDAY
☐	☐	☐	☐	☐	☐	☐
☐	☐	☐	☐	☐	☐	☐
☐	☐	☐	☐	☐	☐	☐
☐	☐	☐	☐	☐	☐	☐
☐	☐	☐	☐	☐	☐	☐
☐	☐	☐	☐	☐	☐	☐

AUGUST CONTENT CALENDAR

MONDAY	TUESDAY	WEDNESDAY	THURSDAY	FRIDAY	SATURDAY	SUNDAY
☐	☐	☐	☐	☐	☐	☐
☐	☐	☐	☐	☐	☐	☐
☐	☐	☐	☐	☐	☐	☐
☐	☐	☐	☐	☐	☐	☐
☐	☐	☐	☐	☐	☐	☐
☐	☐	☐	☐	☐	☐	☐

SEPTEMBER CONTENT CALENDAR

MONDAY	TUESDAY	WEDNESDAY	THURSDAY	FRIDAY	SATURDAY	SUNDAY
☐	☐	☐	☐	☐	☐	☐
☐	☐	☐	☐	☐	☐	☐
☐	☐	☐	☐	☐	☐	☐
☐	☐	☐	☐	☐	☐	☐
☐	☐	☐	☐	☐	☐	☐
☐	☐	☐	☐	☐	☐	☐

OCTOBER CONTENT CALENDAR

MONDAY	TUESDAY	WEDNESDAY	THURSDAY	FRIDAY	SATURDAY	SUNDAY
☐	☐	☐	☐	☐	☐	☐
☐	☐	☐	☐	☐	☐	☐
☐	☐	☐	☐	☐	☐	☐
☐	☐	☐	☐	☐	☐	☐
☐	☐	☐	☐	☐	☐	☐
☐	☐	☐	☐	☐	☐	☐

NOVEMBER CONTENT CALENDAR

MONDAY	TUESDAY	WEDNESDAY	THURSDAY	FRIDAY	SATURDAY	SUNDAY
☐	☐	☐	☐	☐	☐	☐
☐	☐	☐	☐	☐	☐	☐
☐	☐	☐	☐	☐	☐	☐
☐	☐	☐	☐	☐	☐	☐
☐	☐	☐	☐	☐	☐	☐
☐	☐	☐	☐	☐	☐	☐

DECEMBER CONTENT CALENDAR

MONDAY	TUESDAY	WEDNESDAY	THURSDAY	FRIDAY	SATURDAY	SUNDAY
☐	☐	☐	☐	☐	☐	☐
☐	☐	☐	☐	☐	☐	☐
☐	☐	☐	☐	☐	☐	☐
☐	☐	☐	☐	☐	☐	☐
☐	☐	☐	☐	☐	☐	☐
☐	☐	☐	☐	☐	☐	☐

NOTES

space for lists and reflections

Reflect on Your Progress

Reflection helps us determine what we're doing well now and what we want to change in the future. We're always learning as we go and trying new things based on what we learned in the past. This is the growth mindset, which can help you along the way as you take on challenges and changes in digital marketing. Writing your own notes on what you find helpful and interesting as well as your thoughts on how your work is going can help you progress and reach your goals faster. The following pages will help you begin to develop a growth mindset as you develop your notes and reflect on your work.

GROWTH MINDSET

SOMETIMES PERSPECTIVE IS EVERYTHING

Instead of telling yourself:	**Try to tell yourself this:**

I'm not good at this.

I can improve with practice.

Social media is always changing and I can't keep up. It's too difficult and I'm over it.

Social media is going to change. I'm going to try one new feature each month to see what I want to use.

Whenever I get mean comments, or even no comments, I'm wasting my time and my effort.

I'm going to make a plan: I'll answer, ignore, block, or report. I will rework my content to encourage positive interaction.

What is Growth Mindset?

We all have fixed and growth mindset opportunities every day. Fixed mindset is when we tell ourselves we cannot do something. This may be learned from experience or from the actions of others around us. Growth mindset is just the opposite. Growth mindset is when we tell ourselves we can do something and search for what we need to help us accomplish our goals.

NOTES

FILL IN THE CHECKLIST SPACES BELOW WITH TO-DOS, IDEAS, AND
OTHER THINGS YOU WANT TO REMEMBER

☐ _____

☐ _____

☐ _____

☐ _____

☐ _____

☐ _____

☐ _____

☐ _____

☐ _____

☐ _____

☐ _____

NOTES

FILL IN THE CHECKLIST SPACES BELOW WITH TO-DOS, IDEAS, AND
OTHER THINGS YOU WANT TO REMEMBER

- [ ] _____
- [ ] _____
- [ ] _____
- [ ] _____
- [ ] _____
- [ ] _____
- [ ] _____
- [ ] _____
- [ ] _____
- [ ] _____
- [ ] _____

NOTES

FILL IN THE CHECKLIST SPACES BELOW WITH TO-DOS, IDEAS, AND
OTHER THINGS YOU WANT TO REMEMBER

- [ ] _____
- [ ] _____
- [ ] _____
- [ ] _____
- [ ] _____
- [ ] _____
- [ ] _____
- [ ] _____
- [ ] _____
- [ ] _____
- [ ] _____

NOTES

FILL IN THE CHECKLIST SPACES BELOW WITH TO-DOS, IDEAS, AND
OTHER THINGS YOU WANT TO REMEMBER

- [ ] _____
- [ ] _____
- [ ] _____
- [ ] _____
- [ ] _____
- [ ] _____
- [ ] _____
- [ ] _____
- [ ] _____
- [ ] _____
- [ ] _____
- [ ] _____

APPENDIX

examples and ideas

Worked Examples Take the Stress out of Planning

Worked examples show you step by step how to do something, solve a problem, or try something out. This appendix uses eMarketing Director as an example so you can see how one company fills out specific pages of this workbook. You can fill out the workbook in any way that is helpful to you. The following pages are meant to show you one process and serve to get you started with your process.

CAMPAIGN PLANNER - EXAMPLE

1) Choose dates for when you will focus on your campaign.

START DATE

November 1, 2023

END DATE

February 1, 2024

Objective of Campaign: The Goal You Will Reach & How

Goal - Start my marketing

How - Introduce my audience to the new workbook!

2) Write something that clearly states your ultimate goal for the campaign.

Milestones to Make it Happen

Finish and publish workbook

Write posts about the workbook on personal accounts

Set up online advertising for the workbook

3) List your benchmarks - what you can do to know you've made progress.

Task	Assigned to	Done
Finish and publish workbook	*Susan*	✓
Take 20-50 photos of the workbook	*Jared*	✓
Complete 3-5 videos about the workbook	*Susan*	
Post regularly to 3 social media platforms	*Abby*	✓
Share with 5 people & ask for reviews	*Susan*	

Notes

4) List tasks here that can help you reach the objective. Be specific, use numbers, and celebrate when you complete each one.

5) Try to delegate! Sometimes it isn't possible, but employees, interns, friends, or family may be able to help you complete a task.

JANUARY CONTENT PLANNER - EXAMPLE

MAIN FOCUS -

Introduce my Audience to the New Workbook

1) Align your content with your campaign.

2) Brainstorm opportunities for content and how you can connect with your audience.

WEEK 1

1. Happy New Year!
2. Post content about the workbook
3. Introduce myself
4. Post happy reviews

WEEK 2

1. Spotlight specific ways the workbook can help people.
2. Post about winter season

WEEK 3

1. MLK Day
2. Feature a customer using the workbook to help run their business

WEEK 4

1. Post content about preparing for the next month
2. Use trending music to make a post about the workbook

To-do list

- Ask for reviews ✓
- Take pictures of book ☐
- Take videos of Susan ☐
- Write 2 blog posts ☐
- Find New Year Quotes ✓
- MLK Day photo ☐
- Winter time photos ☐
- ☐
- ☐
- ☐
- ☐
- ☐
- ☐
- ☐
- ☐

3) List all the things you need to create your content ideas.

4) Write what you want to do this month for your content. Give yourself more details so you can keep creating!

Notes

This month I want to post to LinkedIn each week with a blog or share a review of the workbook. I also want to put my content on instagram and highlight how staying organized can help you start the new year right!

JANUARY CONTENT CALENDAR

1) Start by recognizing holidays and important dates.

MONDAY	TUESDAY	WEDNESDAY	THURSDAY	FRIDAY	SATURDAY	SUNDAY
☐ 1 Happy New Year Post	☐ 2	☐ 3 Introducing eMarketing Director	☐ 4 Celebrate the New Year Graphic	☐ 5	☐ 6	☐ 7 **2) Vary the days and times of posts to learn what gets the most engagement.**
☐ 8 New Year New Goals Video	☐ 9	☐ 10 Why it's Important to Organize Social Media	☐ 11	☐ 12 Top 3 Ways to Organize Social Media	☐ 13 Social Media Doesn't Take a Break, But You Should	☐ 14
☐ 15 Happy MLK Day Post	☐ 16 Featured Workbook User #1 Story	☐ 17 Link to Purchase Workbook	☐ 18	☐ 19 Yay, it's Friday Post	☐ 20	☐ 21
☐ 22 Repost: Why it's Important to Organize Social Media	☐ 23	☐ 24 Featured Workbook User #2 Story	☐ 25	☐ 26 How to Avoid the "Sunday Scaries"	☐ 27	☐ 28
☐ 29	☐ 30 Repost: Link to Purchase Workbook	☐ 31 Planning for Next Month	☐	☐	**3.) Post several days ahead of schedule for an event or themed post so it has time to show up on newsfeeds.**	
4.) Consider reposting earlier content from the month to recycle your work and make it easier on yourself!			☐	☐	☐	☐

Congratulations! (You Made It!)

Congratulations! This page brings us to the end of the the workbook! Now don't stop here. You can continue to plan, research, act, and reflect on your social media marketing. There are eMarketing Director resources to follow, but also be sure to explore the social media platform websites themselves. Many have specific pages for businesses and creators. The more opportunities you give yourself to practice and work towards your goals the better you will feel and the closer you will be to reaching your goals. To learn more, ask questions, and connect to our community visit www.emarketingdirector.com.

ABOUT THE AUTHOR

Dr. Susan Fant Cassity founded eMarketing Director to help people take the stress out of their digital marketing, so they can reach their goals and then go back to doing what they love to do (instead of worrying about likes, shares, and all the changes being made on the platforms). Susan is the owner of two companies and she created one of the first digital and social media marketing specializations at the Master's of Marketing level in the USA at the University of Alabama. Susan earned degrees and certifications in business, entrepreneurship, creative industries, and organizational change and leadership from Birmingham-Southern College, University of St Andrews, Stanford University, Cornell University, and the University of Southern California.

You can learn more about Susan and contact her directly at www.emarketingdirector.com.

Made in the USA
Columbia, SC
16 May 2024

35722276R00080